# Starting to Read
# with Sniffer

## Book 1 This is Sniffer

Pippa Pennington

Illustrated by Eitatsu

It is recommended that you begin with Book 1. To help your child learn initial reading skills, talk about the picture first. Then follow the text with your finger under each word as you read.

Reading and story time is about enjoyment and installing a love of books into your child. The more you read together, the more he or she will learn.

All children learn at different times. Let them read at their own pace, when they are ready.

The Starting to Read with Sniffer series are books for beginners and will give your child good recognition skills for reading keywords which will constantly appear in their reading books.

The Starting to Read series is complimented by the Sniffer Rhyming Books series. When children become familiar with Sniffer and his antics, they will be eager to join in and pre-empt the words.

These early learning books for beginner readers will give a good foundation on which to build reading skills. The simple vocabulary includes high frequency words from The National Curriculum keywords which are essential for beginner readers.

Sniffer

This is Sniffer

This is Sniffer.

This is Sniffer.

This is Sniffer.

Here is Sniffer.

Here is Sniffer.

Sniffer is here.

Sniffer is here.

Sniffer is here.

nose

nose

This is Sniffer's nose.

tail

tail

This is Sniffer's tail.

Sniffer's tail wags.

Sniffer's tail wags.

Sniffer's tail wags.

Sniffer wags his tail.

Sniffer is happy.

Sniffer is happy.

Sniffer wags his tail when he is happy.

Sniffer's tail is not wagging.

# Free Book

Get your free rhyming eBook,

Phew! What's that smell?

Join my reading group for news of new releases, offers, and other goodies.

https://rhyme1.adventureswithsniffer.com/

I'll send your eBook to keep as a thank you and you can unsubscribe at any time.

Sniffer, Sniffer at the Beach, Sniffer at the Farm, Sniffer's First Christmas, and Sniffer goes on holiday, are suitable for young children to listen, beginners to join in, and the familiar text encourages children to read alone. Picture recognition will support reading skills, but children will soon discover that the words have to be read as the pictures are similar across all Sniffer books.

When the words in Starting to Read with Sniffer are read with confidence, play a game. For word recognition, out of the context of this book, write one word from each page onto a piece of paper. Can he or she see the same word on the page? Can they say the word? Turn the words over so they can't be seen. Can they choose one and find the word in the book? Can they say the word?

A happy child is a learning child.

# Other books by Pippa Pennington

## Picture Books

Sniffer: the little dog who likes to sniff

Sniffer at the Beach

Sniffer at the Farm

Sniffer's First Christmas

Sniffer goes on Holiday

## Sniffer Rhyming Books (these run alongside the picture books)

Phew! What's that smell? (Book 1)

Phew! What's that smell at the Beach? (Book 2)

Phew! What's that smell at the Farm? (Book 3)

Phew! What's that smell at Christmas? (Book 4)

Phew! What's that smell on Holiday? (Book 5)

The rhyming books have been written to enhance the reading experience. The repeated vocabulary will give children confidence when they begin to read for themselves. Visit https://www.pippapennington.co.uk for tips on helping your child to read.

## Starting to read with Sniffer

Book 2 Sniffer likes...

Book 3 Sniffer can see...

Book 4 Sniffer can smell...

Book 5 Who is this?

Printed in Great Britain
by Amazon

61371482R00017